BOOK 2 • ELEMENTARY

PIANO *for* TWO

DUETS EQUAL PARTS FOR ONE PIANO, 4 HANDS

arranged by
Carol Matz

Production: Frank and Gail Hackinson
Production Coordination and Text Design: Marilyn Cole
Editors: Victoria McArthur and Edwin McLean
Cover: Terpstra Design, San Francisco
Engraving: GrayBear Music Company, Hollywood, Florida
Printer: Tempo Music Press, Inc.

THE
F·J·H
MUSIC
COMPANY
INC.

A Note to Teachers

Most students find duet playing to be a fun and challenging addition to their everyday piano studies. Duets offer students a chance to learn from the experience of making music with another person. **Piano For Two**® provides a wonderful opportunity for students to work on aspects of ensemble playing, such as dynamic balance and tempo control, while learning some of their favorite well-known pieces.

In these arrangements, simple eighth note rhythms are used, but dotted-quarter and more sophisticated rhythms are avoided. Although hand movement is kept to a minimum, circled finger numbers signal any change of position.

Fore easier reading, one or both parts call for an octave transposition, which is clearly marked in the score. Additionally, in many instances the melody shifts between *primo* and *secondo*, affording the opportunity to work on dynamic blending.

Piano For Two® is available in six volumes, ranging in difficulty from early elementary through late intermediate/advanced levels. Students will be delighted by the variety of pieces included in each book, representing the classics, well-known favorites, original pieces, and more.

CONTENTS

The Stars and Stripes Forever 4

Simple Gifts 8

La Cinquantaine *(The Golden Wedding)* 12

Home on the Range 16

Dance of the Sugar-Plum Fairy 20

Mexican Festival 24

Dictionary of Musical Terms 28

The Stars and Stripes Forever

Secondo

John Philip Sousa

The Stars and Stripes Forever

Primo

John Philip Sousa

Moderate march tempo

(Play both hands 1 octave higher)

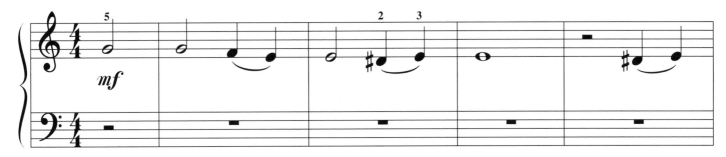

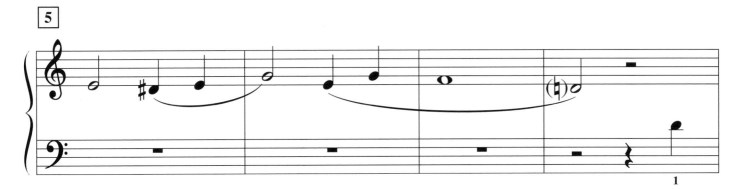

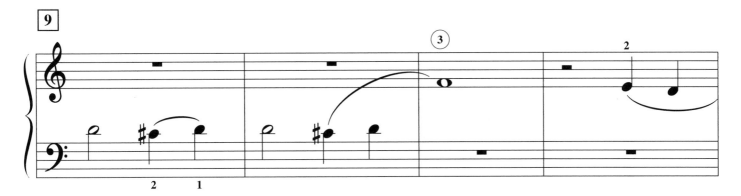

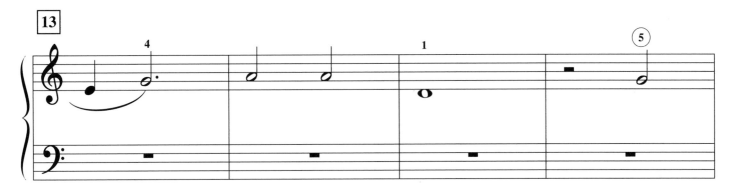

FF1146

Secondo

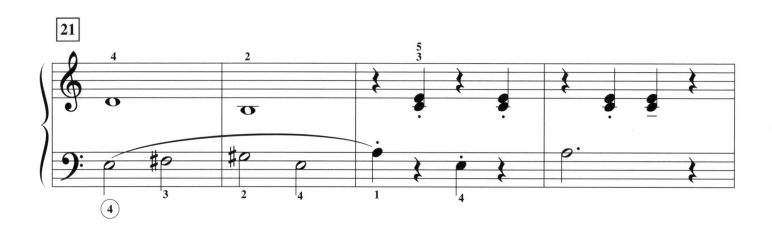

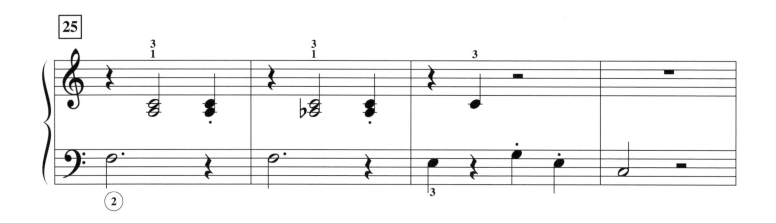

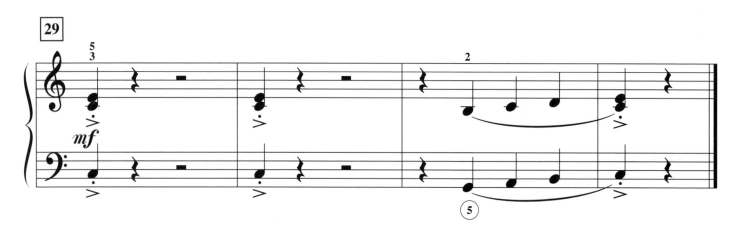

Primo

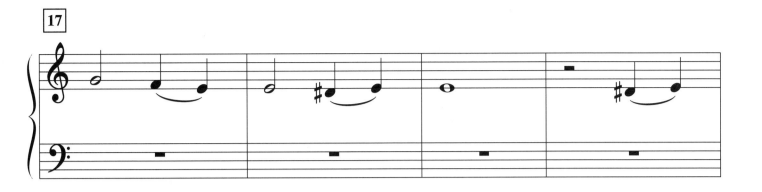

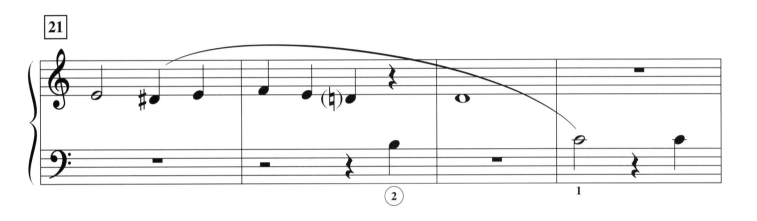

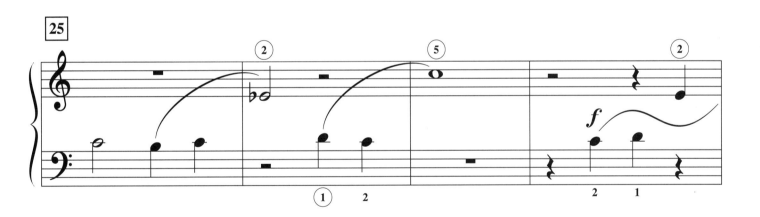

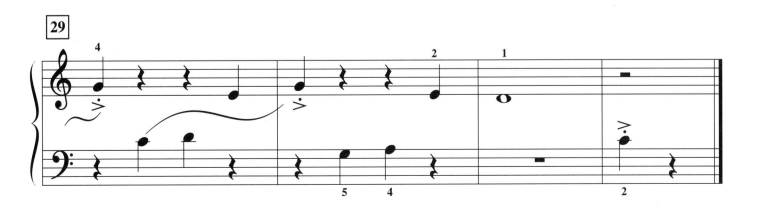

Simple Gifts

Secondo

Traditional Shaker song

Flowing

(Play both hands 1 octave lower)

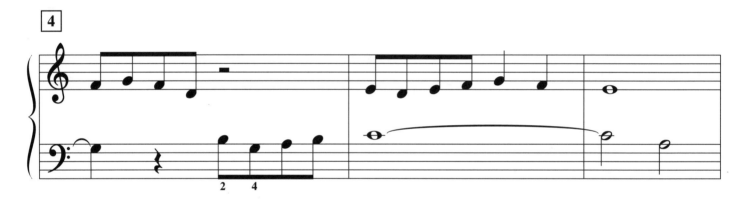

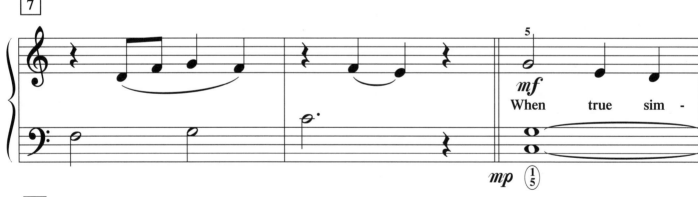

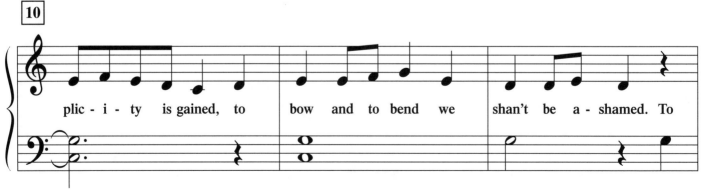

Simple Gifts

Primo

Traditional Shaker song

Flowing

(Play both hands 1 octave higher)

'Tis the gift to be sim- ple, 'tis the gift to be free, 'tis the gift to come down

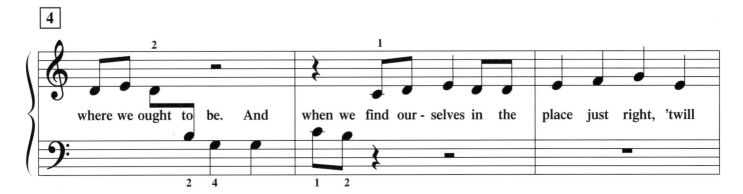

where we ought to be. And when we find our - selves in the place just right, 'twill

be in the val - ley of love and de - light.

FF1146

Secondo

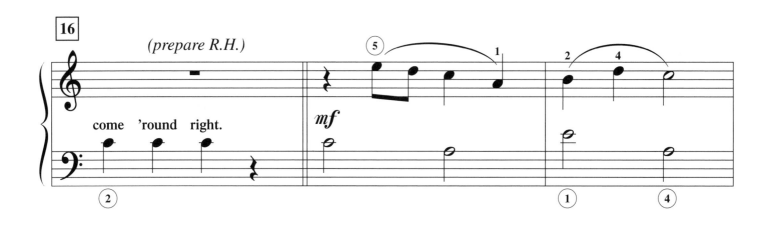

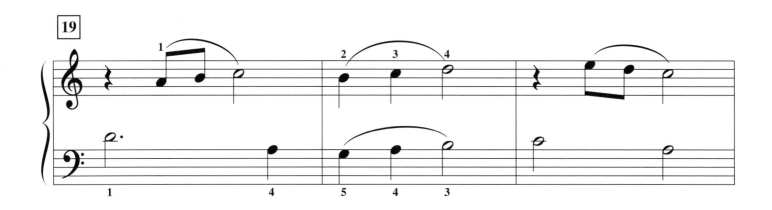

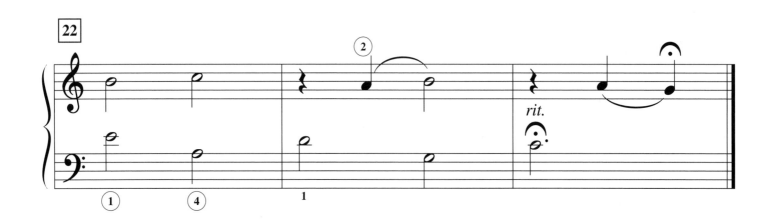

Primo

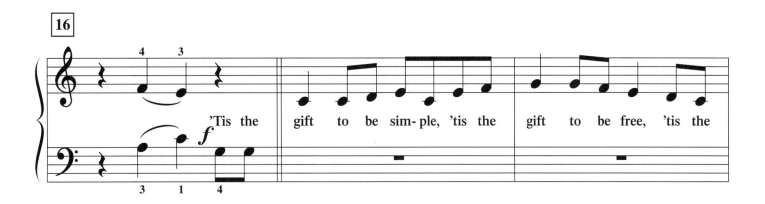

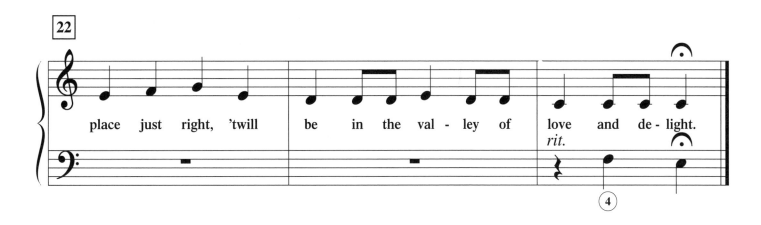

La Cinquantaine
(The Golden Wedding)
Secondo

Gabriel-Marie

Moderately fast

(Play both hands 1 octave lower)

La Cinquantaine
(The Golden Wedding)
Primo

Gabriel-Marie

Moderately fast

(Play both hands 1 octave higher)

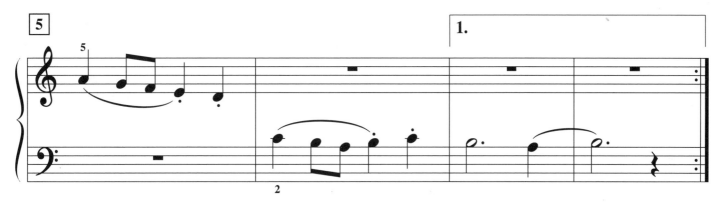

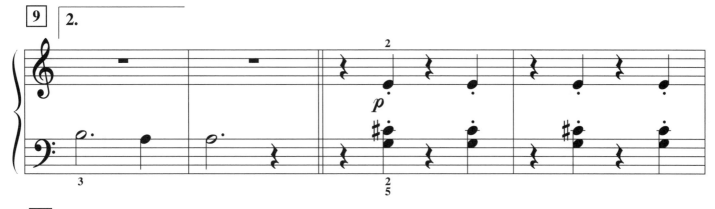

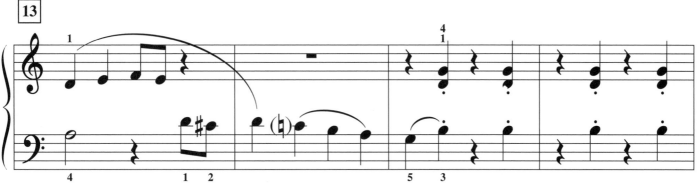

FF1146

Secondo

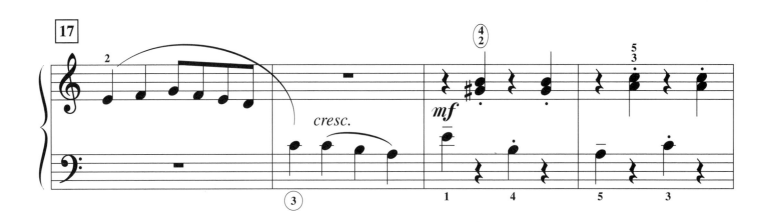

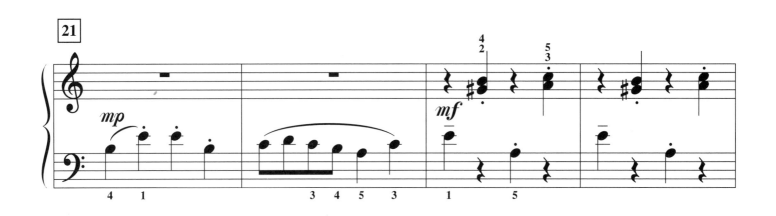

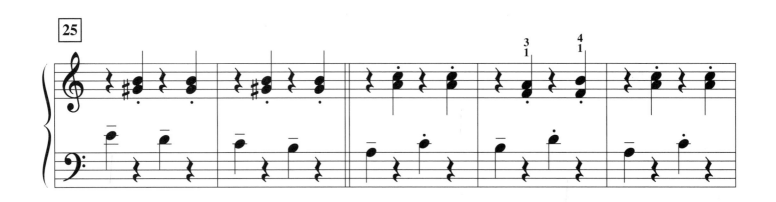

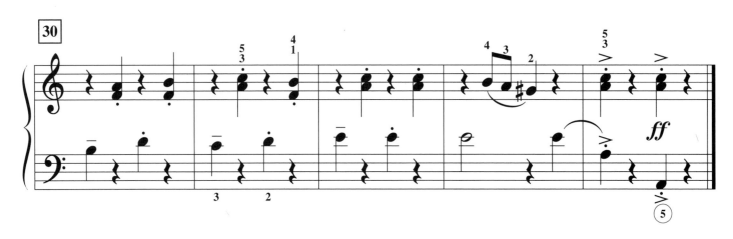

Primo

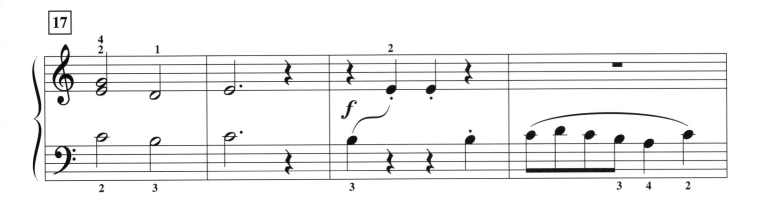

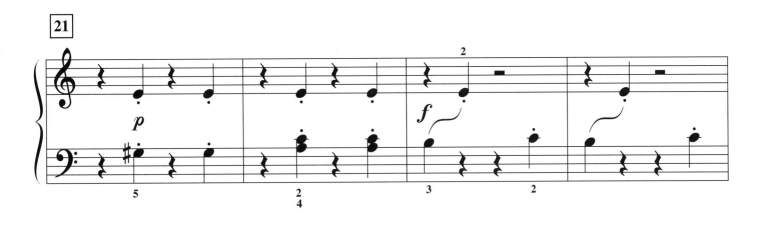

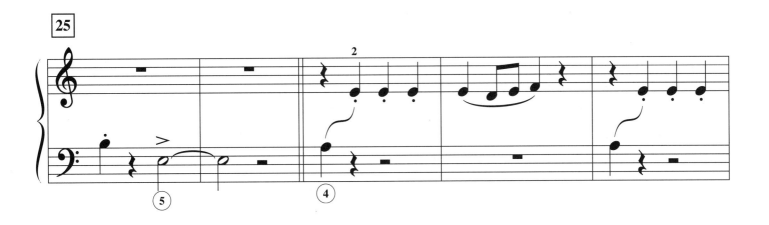

Home on the Range

Secondo

American Folk song

Smoothly

(Play both hands 1 octave lower)

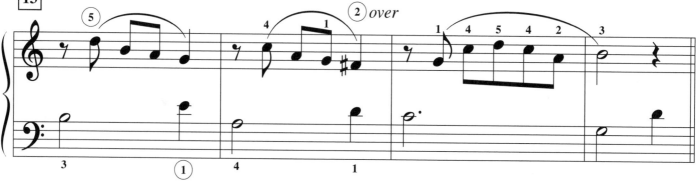

Home on the Range

Primo

American Folk song

Smoothly

(Play both hands 1 octave higher)

Secondo

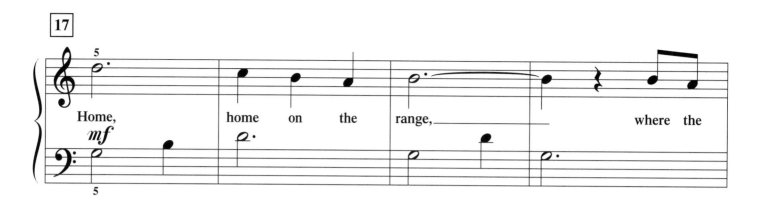

Home, home on the range,_____ where the

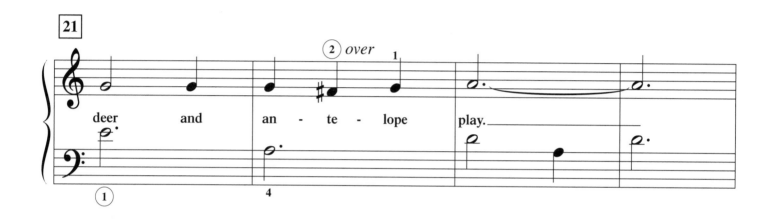

deer and an - te - lope play._____

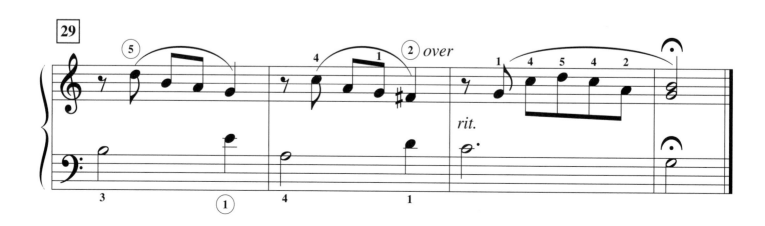

Primo

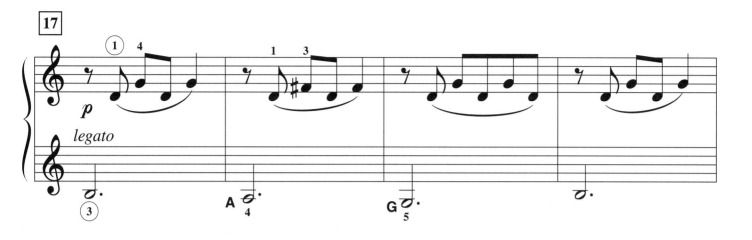

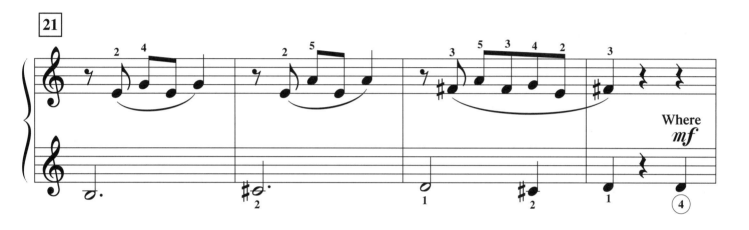

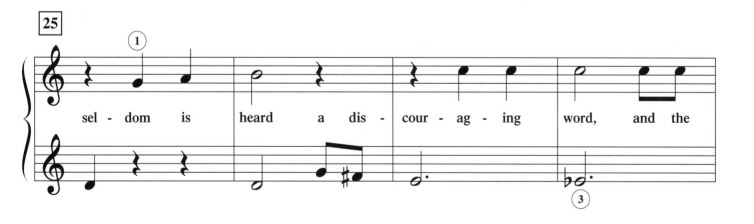

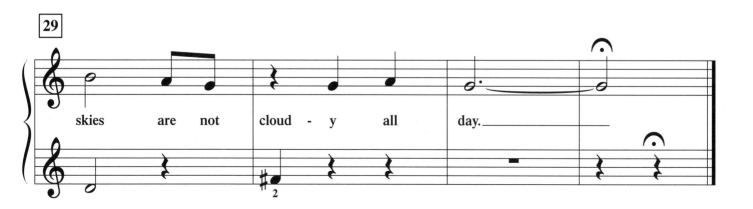

Dance of the Sugar-Plum Fairy
(from The Nutcracker)
Secondo

Peter Ilyich Tchaikovsky

Mysteriously

(Play as written)

Dance of the Sugar-Plum Fairy
(from The Nutcracker)
Primo

Peter Ilyich Tchaikovsky

Mysteriously

(Play both hands 2 octaves higher)

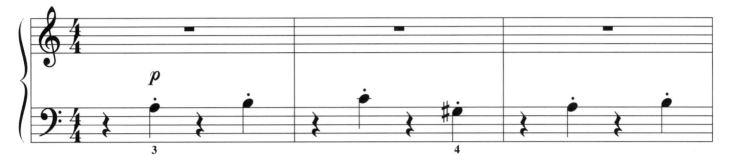

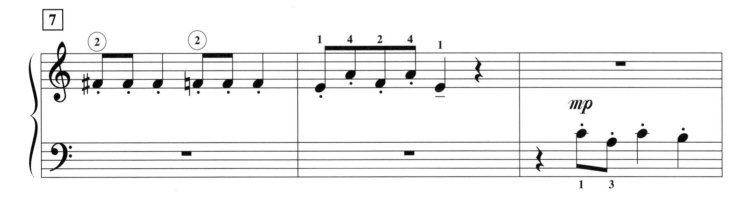

FF1146

Secondo

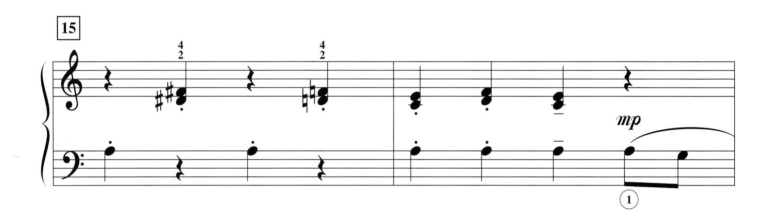

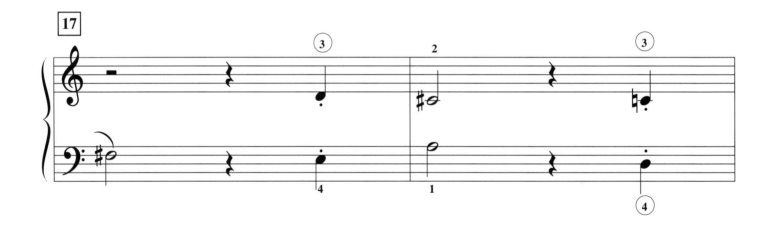

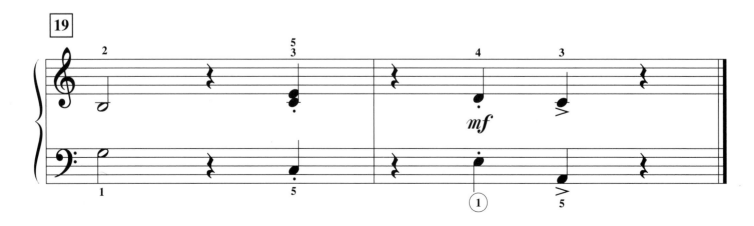

Primo

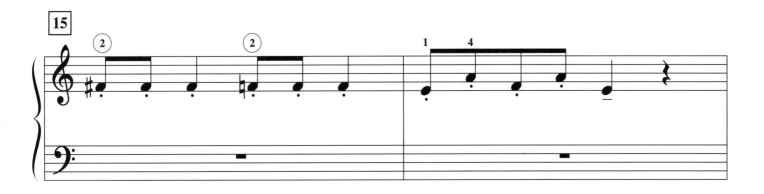

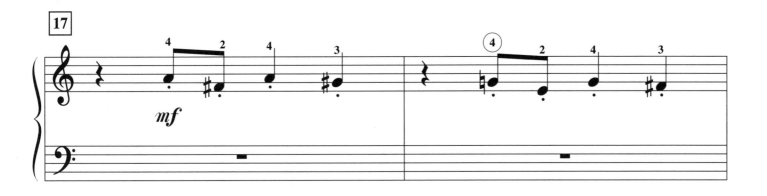

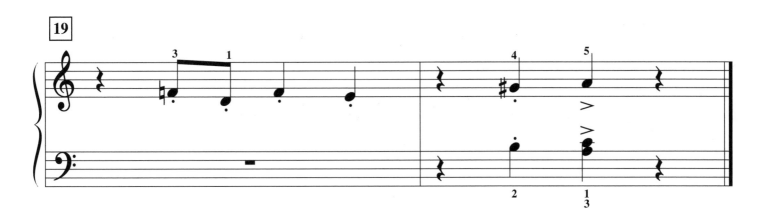

Mexican Festival

Secondo

Carol Matz

Moderately fast

(Play both hands 1 octave lower)

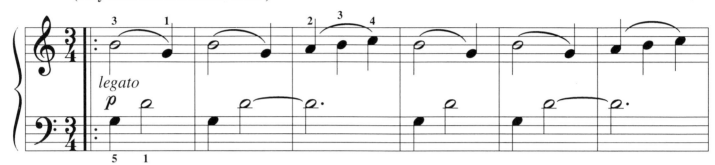

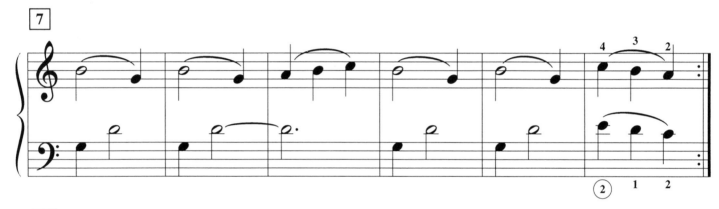

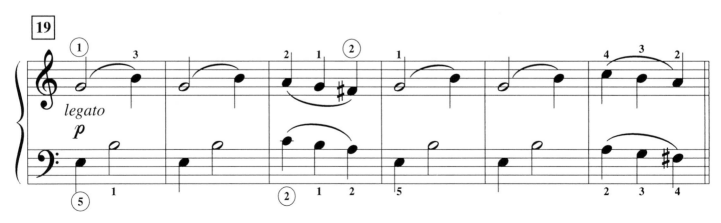

Mexican Festival

Primo

Carol Matz

Moderately fast

(Play both hands 1 octave higher)

FF1146

Secondo

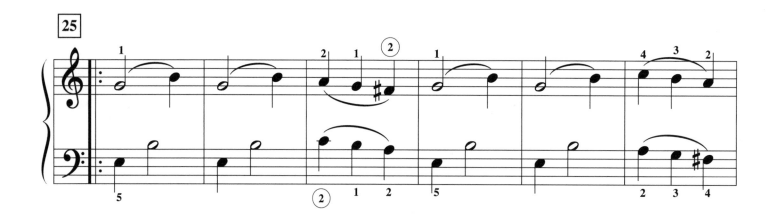

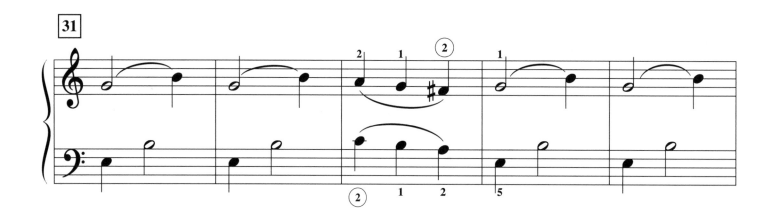

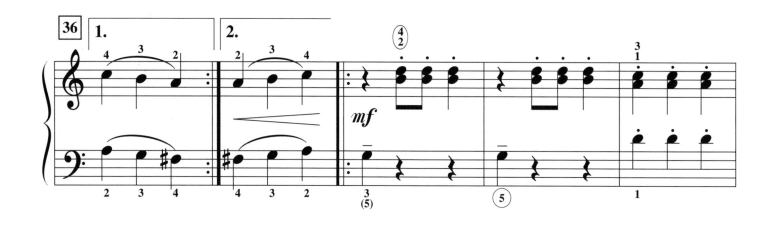

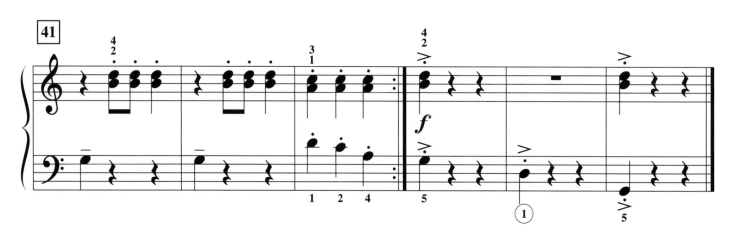

Primo

Dictionary of Musical Terms

(staccato note)	*staccato*	Play the note short and detached.
(accent note)	**accent**	Play an accented note louder, with emphasis.
(tenuto note)	*tenuto*	A slight stress. (Also known as a *stress mark*.)
(slur notes)	**slur**	Play these notes connected, smoothly.
rit.	*ritardando*	Slow down gradually.
(fermata)	*fermata*	Hold the note longer than usual.
(repeat signs)	**repeat signs**	Play the music between the repeat signs twice.
1. 2.	**1st and 2nd endings**	Play the 1st ending, then take the repeat. Then play the 2nd ending in place of the 1st ending.
	legato	Play smoothly.
	octave	A distance of 8 scale tones higher or lower. (Ex.: C up to C; F down to F.)
	Primo	The first part in a duet. Refers to the music for the player sitting on the right.
	Secondo	The second part in a duet. Refers to the music for the player sitting on the left.

Dynamic Symbols

pp (*pianissimo*) . . . . .very soft		***mf*** (*mezzo-forte*) . . . . .medium loud	
p (*piano*) . . . . .soft		***f*** (*forte*) .loud	
mp (*mezzo-piano*) . . . . .medium soft		***ff*** (*fortissimo*) . . . . .very loud	

crescendo (*cresc.*)
play louder gradually

diminuendo (*dim.*)
play softer gradually